THE BOOK OF SONGS

BY

ROHSAD C. FARAJ

About the Author

Rohsad is a rapper, songwriter, producer and an inspired book writer. His music captivates listeners in a rare and powerful wave that sets him apart from others musical artists. Rohsad is attempting to release his powerful lyrics into a book for his fan to read. His rap and writing style is born out of pain, struggles, love and passion for music. In the year 2021, Rohsad made his introduction into the music scene with two (2) anticipated music albums. One of which is entitled "The struggle."- a creative and compelling album that guarantees satisfaction to all music lovers. In 2025, Rohsad is set to release a book version of his lyrics for readers. Rohsad grew up in Bronx, New York, the birth place of Hip Hop. He wanted to become a rapper and a book writer while pursuing a Bachelor's degree from the State University of New York at Buffalo. Rohsad is self-taught when it comes to rapping and song writing. His unique style of writing songs started to take roots after experiencing unemployment and homelessness.

Dedication

I dedicate this book to my God, my constant source of strength, love, and guidance. Through every joy and every sorrow, You have never left my side. In my moments of doubt, You gave me hope. In my struggles, You lifted me up. Without You, this journey would not have been possible.

Thank You for Your endless grace, for every blessing, and for always being there.

Contents

1

Girl, You're A Winner.

Like two best friends, it's good when we talk.
Yes, you impress me with the way you walk.
You can make it on your own. You're not afraid to work. We're
both from New York. Teamwork makes it work.
Don't be too shy; it's me that you like?
What is it look like? Tell me if your type.
You're such a good sight on this special night.
Your vibes are alright. We went over some miles.
Flash me that smile. Yes, it is so fine.
Your whole profile is just wild style.
I do like the way you move, and you are so smooth.
This is a hot date, we are doing so great.
The next move you and I are ready to make. The dessert will be
this nice sweet cake.

Like camera lenses, my focus is on you.
You are skillful. I know what you could do.
Spin it. Work it. Yeah, I do love it.
After a good break, we're getting back with it.
Here we go! Let's go!
Good one! Hot move! That's awesome, baby!
You're doing good tricks. That's surprising, baby.
There you go! Drop it low!
I want more. That's for sure.
I grab your waist. You do that twist. You bite your lips. I love them
hips.
I like how you react. Give me more of that.
Oh, you're throwing it back!

Yeah, you're throwing it back.

Do more of that touching. Do more of that grabbing. I will keep on pushing. Our bodies are moving. Both of us are going for a cool, hot ending.

2
You're Charming

You're looking really confident, strolling in this hot zone.
You have plenty of good moves. So, you could just go on.
You can climb on top. I feel the sensation, when you put the
pressure on. Yeah, you got me turned on.
We could make this last long, up till the break of dawn.
We could let it be known from this day on; we are moving as one.
With you, things are so on. You're dealing with a champion.
You could definitely be one: cool, collected, and calm.
Accept my invitation. Welcome to my hot zone. Some call it the
love zone.
You might be the right one to light my fire on.
Attention! Affection! I give them in my love zone.
I like how you whisper with a nice low tone.
Letting out some soft moans. To you, I am so drawn.
Let the flames spark on. Let us both rock on.
This is pure seduction. A whole night session.
We could just restart. Ok, we are back on.
Once again, and again, you know I am so on. Touchdown in the
hot zone!

You're awesome. I want some. That move is a good one.
That might be my favorite one.
Do that more till it's enough.
You can be a little rough. You know I will not break.
I am built a little tough. Back it up. Throw it up. I'll catch up.
That's no bluff. You sure have some good stuff.
Like I drink a love potion, I just can't leave you alone.

We find good angles and positions. We're going back and forth
with the motions. I'm swimming in that warm ocean.
You can come at me strong while playing your favorite song.
Pleasing you, I'm all about. Yes, I like to work it out.
Girl, you know I choose you for this midnight rendezvous.
I might just surprise you. We're inside; lock the doors.
That's for sure. I want more.
We do it with passion. Plus, a lot of actions.
We both have good reasons to do it all seasons.
It could be day or night; we both could make it hot.

3
I'm Ready

Go ahead, baby; work your charm on me. I want to see you happy.
You should smile for me. Try this outfit for me.
You're looking so tasty. Come on, then approach me. Don't be
afraid to touch me. You can bet on me to make you feel worthy.
You put that move on me. Now, I am feeling lucky. You're about
to show me what I'm missing lately. Oh yeah, jackpot! That's the
spot? Really! Yeah, you really got me. Keep it going, baby. I want
that daily. My appetite is healthy. If you want to be the energizer
bunny, that is fine with me. Switch it up; twist it up and stir it up,
baby. You can bring it to me.
I will keep up, baby. I'm the marathon lover. I'm the all-night
worker. I'm the slow or fast goer. I aim to please you, baby. I'm like
a genie. I'm at your service, baby. That's a guarantee. You can be
creative and make it hot and spicy. Do it all over whenever you're
ready.

Come and give it to me if you are ready. You could just surprise
me. Try your new moves on me. Your style could be low-key or
even flashy. We could work it slowly. Or we could speed it up.
Okay, try me. The test is going nicely. At times, it is bumpy and
outright shaky. Grab me, squeeze me. I'm pushing it steady.
Smoothly or roughly. On and on we carry. We make it our duty to
really go heavy. Satisfaction for me is when you talk back to me
while throwing it at me. It's always good to see you working that
body. Girl, you do it for me. I'm glad that you picked me.
Experiment on me.
Like, you're my favorite nurse. I like your good therapy. That is
your specialty.

Like a good waitress, you know how to serve me.
You have good skills that really come in handy.
Let's go for another round.
It's really plain to see that I am ready.

4
I Have To Carry On

It's a worldwide paper chase. I don't mind starting the race. Millionaire ambition that's the real truth in my case. Entrepreneur with a dream, I'm going at a fast pace. I'm moving like the speed of sound for the bread and the cake. I'm giving you some classic hits. I'm a music heavyweight. Label me a professional; you can bet my work is great. You can tell from head to toe that I'm a man of real taste. I believe in success. All the best moves I will make. So, what if you are full of hate. Choke with hate and suffocate. You have a crab-in-the-bucket mindset. It's so sad! You're a waste. Let's talk about breadwinning. I don't have time for playing. I don't mind doing hard work to have big steaks on my plate. I bring fierce competition. I'm ready to dominate. I will be the people's champ; I can't wait to celebrate. This is my big chess move. You have realized too late; that this game is so over. This is a real checkmate.

I work hard to get paid up. It's only right, I move up. My style so well built up. How you're going to break it up? Like a great heavy steel, it will always hold up. Selective, the architect. It's good music that I construct. Guarantee satisfaction; come check out my good product. I'm putting work that's long lasting and I don't mind winning. I will keep on inventing. This music craft I'm mastering. I want to owe businesses that provide good services. I'll make all you haters scream out! I want time out! Break your back, make you fall out. I want my work to spread out. I want my team to have mass clout. You can tell by the way I move that I'll be on a mission. It's a fact!
I have been conditioned to lockdown any position. Time for me to think wise and have my own business enterprise.

7

5
Turn Me On

I am at my prime. I am at my best. Baby, be my guest in this dance contest.

Speed it up. Slow it down and make me scream yes. You're moving up and down. You're looking mighty fine. Yes, I must confess. I am feeling real blessed. The way we're moving, everybody impress. Greenlight, you should go. I am watching you go. You're moving like a pro. That's really dope yo. Shake it up. Stir it up. Go a little harder. Move that thing faster. Temperature goes higher when you move up closer. It's a music fest. I'll put you up to the test. With that real cute dress, show me what you got next. Side to side, break it down, and all around, yeah. Sexiest, meanest, and NYC's finest. You're looking the nicest. On you I will invest, quality time I suggest. Checkout in progress. We're driving and heading west! We are going express.

You really have good taste. This is your showcase. You're moving with good grace at an awesome pace. Bring it on. Turn me on. Ok, it's on. You can come at me strong. I could make it last long. I could work you out. Hours and hours long. It is highly likely that you will want me. Yes, you can trust me to give it to you daily. Anytime you need me, you can have me, baby. We're off to a good start; take your clothes off slowly. My massage therapy will get you hooked thoroughly. Good body working. You're adrenaline-rushing. It is perfect timing for your climaxing. I could put work in the morning till its evening. You might just start saying, dady, dady, dady. You I am keeping.

6
Here

Music is my life. My life is music. That's the real reason that I am here. Let me be really clear. Music is the latter for me to climb up here. Open up your ears. This message you should hear. I have the vision of becoming a boss here. Even if it's hard work, I will make some bread here. This is how I'm thinking, I'm with empire building, dynasty running, really make it big here. Like a real legend, I will make my mark here. Yes, my plan will work here. I need my team in here. Money to be made here. Let's handle business here. Yeah, I'm on my grind here. Like you hit the lotto, I'll make you feel good here. I give you quality hits to hypnotize here. That's the real proof here. I'll get you in the zone here. Music playing, body shaking, rock with me in here.

I'm sharpen up my skills. I could set some trends. I'm a modern-day inventor. I'm out for their ends. I might drive a Lexus. Yes, I do like Benz. BMW, too, I could get used to. I have appetite for good things. My taste will not change. Don't you look at me strangely for wanting some fine things? Every day I wake up, I'm looking to move up. Finding ways to cake up. I'll go Up! I mean, moving way up. I have business numbers on my phone to dial. Green papers, I must have. Let it pile for a while. Yes, I must confess. I don't mind success. On myself, I'll invest. I have a Wall Street mindset when it comes to my nest. Extra! Extra! Here comes the next real bet. I will become a rider and ride to sunset.

7

To God, You Should Huddle

You should always praise the Lord.
He's mightier than a sword.
The enemy crumbles when he utters one word.
When you are feeling weak.
It's the Lord you should seek.
Every day, worship him. He does hear when you speak.
Call on the God, almighty, when your load is too heavy.
Your burden he will carry. Your safety is guaranteed.
Trust the Lord, don't you worry.
He'll crush the Devil's army.
Have them flee in a hurry.
Give the Lord all the glory.
He's full of might and power.
At the darkest of hours.
He will be your protector.
He's always your Savior.
In the Lord, you should have faith; become a true believer,
follower, and worshipper.
He knows all your wants and needs.
He's your greatest provider.
He is the best counselor and a wonderful master.
There is no one that's greater.

The Lord is your companion. He's your heavyweight champion.
He's the source of your blessings. There is no time for wasting.
To him, you should be running. The Lord is always Growing.
His power has no ending.
Always stand up for your Lord. Meditate on all his words.

You can count on your Great Lord.

When the demons try you out, he will cast the devils out.

You should have no fear and doubt. Praise his holy name and shout.

The Lord is your redeemer. He's a heart and soul cleanser.

The Lord can make you prosper. He's the greatest life changer. His power is forever.

Even in the battlefield, the Lord is your greatest shield.

Always carry out his will. His promise he will fulfill.

Through your trials and struggles with the Lord, you stay faithful.

Never side with the Devil. He is wicked and evil.

He brings nothing but trouble. The Lord is well capable of punishing the Devil.

Really, on the double, to the Lord, you should huddle.

8
That's What It Is

I could think on my own, yeah, you know that's what's up.
Now my eyes are open up. Like a helicopter, I want to move way
up. I know how to construct. I'm a modern-day architect; yes, I
want to build up. I'm a musical engineer. I want to get paid up. I
will shred this beat up and make you just jump up. You might give
me two thumbs up. Like a July summer, I will turn the heat up.
That's for sure; why not? Selective is a hot shot! You're
temperature, I'll raise it up. That's the latter of success? Yes, I want
to climb up.
Up! Up! Yeah! East, West, North, South.
Yes, I want to move up. Like every day is my birthday; yes, I want
to cake up. For everything that I have lost, now, I want to grab up.
Fast or slow, either; you can bet I'll come up. Money, I will make it
up. Like applying makeup, you could say he's changing up. Shower
me with that green. Like a pool, fill it up. For sure, I will swim up.
With wealth, I want to catch up. I'm not thinking of slowing up.
I'm thinking of speeding up, right on the target. Give it up! No
way, I will pass that up!

I might just shake things up and have you raise your hands up.
Ladies, you could just walk up and really turn it up. Let me see,
pop that up. Oh yeah, you can stir it up. I like how you keep it up.
I'm glad that I picked you up. You and I can team up and really
mix things up. Get the crowd all hype up. So, let's just blaze it up.
You know we are high up. Let's do more and go up. Like it is
fireworks, I want this place to light up.
This is my next step up. Climb the latter and move up. Like the
pizza-making man, it's a whole lot of dough that I want to touch

up. Stretch them out and spread them up. From the ground up, I'll really stock my chips up. I will get my weight up and really push them bars up.

9

Lift Your Hands Up People

Even when I lay low at night in the shadows. My dreams turn in circles. Going in slow-mo. How I'm going to stop? They're so hard not to follow. Bigger do they grow, make me want to scream whoa! What if I just blow? All the higher I'll go. I'm putting out good shows. Get my hands on more dough. My money will sure grow. If you do want my flow. You pay me upfront, yo. I do good with promos. I'll make it a hot show and turn up the tempo. You know I'm a real pro. Go to the next level. This is a real show. Nobody moving slow, I'm looking at the crowd go. This is so official. This moment is special. I will not let it go. Oh wow, here we go! Them girls got the flow. Move your hips and wine slow. All night we can go. You're coming back for more. Alright, let's go!

Alright. Ready? Get set. Let's go! I know what you go for. I could provide you more.
This is what you came for; you walked through the right door.
Take the stress off your chest and dance a little more.
You can rock back and forth, even at your tables. Giving you the right music, of that I'm capable. Ok. For sure. You can hit the dance floor. Left, right, go down, pop up, fast or slow. Stir it up and let them know. You can do it like a pro. Now, the time has come for the Selective show. The distance I will go. I write music on the go; And let my skills show. I am really able to give you a showdown and keep it lyrical. Negative attention that I don't care for. All the hate I ignore. I go above and do more. I drop rhymes that are hot, like an inferno. Music is my dojo. Here's the next thing you should know. My flow can be lethal.

10
Quality Hits

I am a professional who really likes to construct. Master of the music craft, check out my good product. Guaranteed satisfaction, you might get addicted. In your house or in your car, play it and get blasted. At any given time for sure, your head will be nodding. Become my number-one fan; I'm good at supplying quality hits. Like a helicopter, I'll take you much higher. I want my music playing inside your house in the near future. My music should multiply and distribute worldwide. The truth I will not hide. You might play it nonstop in your drop-top car, and You might just scream out, he's really hot!
You know that I'll make it hot. Selective, he don't stop. Yes, I'm aiming for the top. I'll make it a good shot, like a telescopic red dot. I want your eardrums on lock; back and forth, you should rock. I will have you feeling nice, like a good drink with ice. My talent is high price. You're getting the right prize.

My rhymes run real deep, like the veins inside you. This is no voodoo, but I got lyrics that I cast spells through. You can feel the impact when it really hits you. I will not blame you if it overwhelms you.
This is really for you. If you like to grind too. Here's another hot verse you could just rock to. Like the mailman, you know I will come through and deliver it for you. It's Like hydraulics, my music you could bounce to. I have something to tell you. Haters I outgrew. Salute to you if you feel the same too. Go ahead. It's on you. Bust a move or two. Solo or with your crew, show them what you can do. That's it, do you? I will continue. I'm on a mission too. That is to rock steady and kick them hot lyrics that stick to you like glue.

11
Take Flight

Grow yourself to be real mighty and powerful.
This life is beautiful. Work hard to be faithful.
All the hardships you go through. Always fight to pull through.
Find something you love to do.
You let no one stop you. You make sure it's not harmful.
You should want your belly full. You do know that God loves you.
So why not just be you? You do have a special gift. Go to work and
make it work.
You should try to be at peace and try to be happy. You get to the
finish line is victory. Yes, that's a victory.
Try this method, and you'll see.

What is all this drama? What is all this problem? You just got to go
on. Like camera lenses, you put your focus on. You do have some
real big dreams. Go to work and make them real. Test your might,
see how it feels. Spread your wings and take flight. Keep climbing
up higher. Try to reach a new height.

You make up a real profile! Try to defeat them with a smile. Oh,
they might just call you wild. Show them that you're versatile. You
show them you have good style. You've been a pro for a while.
Nothing wrong with being wise. Keep your eyes on the prize!
Your time is so precious. That's why we should be cautious. They
all could be nervous and talking a lot of mess. Always try to do
your best! Go all out; give it your best!

12

Downtown

Hey baby, certainly, I'm fighting to be free.
Are you coming with me? Are you even with me?
Do you even like me? You know who I might be.
Alright, then, come at me. I have enough energy that will really last me.
Don't you just walk past me? Do you really got me?
Curiosity! You're silly. Why don't you just try me?
I dare you to say gladly. Laughter and laughter.
Oh, I know you're hearing me.
You might want to challenge me and hang out all night with me.
There is food if you're hungry. There is a drink if you're thirsty.
You're looking so stylish with the right outfit and the look is so classy. I want to hug you, really.
You're smelling so good, girl. Things will sure get spicy.
Why don't you get comfortable, play some music, and dance for me?
Oh, you have some good moves! Go ahead, impress me.
I want a nice preview of how it might just be.
You're changing outfits for me. We're both are antsy.
Our blood was boiling with excitement, giddy and bubbly. We're about to get busy.

In this very hard life, you do really stand out.
I like how you're coming out. Confidently, walk it out.
Turnabout. I might shout.
I'm so glad to check you out.
Like you are my favorite dish, you are on my wanted list.
You sure do know how to switch. You look good doing that twist.

Like a magnet, you keep on drawing me, pulling me.
Yes, indeed. You need me. Come tell me.
You can reach out to me. You really will have me.
You are motivating me. Put that good wine on me.
Do it fast or slow for me. Hot rounds! Yeah, you know I got plenty.
Yes, I am ready for what you can show me.
I like how you get busy. Life can be real salty.
Now, you're making it easy. I enjoy your company.
We have some good chemistry. So, let's make it steady.
We can do this alright. Work it out for many nights.

13
Things Will Get Hot

Hey good looking, you are such a pretty sight.
How you're acting is so right.
You get two thumbs up, alright.
Tonight, by the moonlight, your catwalk is real tight.
You could flash me that smile. You got me feeling right.
You're charming, alarming. You know what you're doing. You're
outright provoking, it's smooth how you're talking.
I have a good feeling that you might say something.
Don't be shy, it's alright. Let your true self come out.
On you, I won't run out.
You'll find out; for you, I will go all out.
It is highly likely that you will like me.
Yes, you can trust me to treat you really fairly.
I'm happy with your chemistry. You bring that good energy.
Like a good invention, you are so awesome.
You're a Wonder Woman. With you, things are better.
We could grow stronger and go so much farther, reaching new
heights.
When I see you, baby, it's only right that things will get hot.

I like how you start things up. You set up a good warm-up.
Go ahead and twist it up. I will steadily push it up.
You can bet I will keep up. We can stretch the time up.
Lights on or lights off. We could make things pop off.
All our clothes go off. You have a real nice touch.
I really like it that much. I am hot and bothered. You make me feel
as such.
I'm telling you no bluff. Oh yeah, you could set it off.

Slow, fast, or even rough. I know you are built tough.
Of you, I can't get enough. With you, it's so on again.
You give me the reason. I want you all seasons.
That's without a question. I like all the actions.
We're both on a mission for a good explosion.
For sure, we could work it out. The soft moans you're letting out
make me want to max it out.
Let another round begin; this is not yet the end.

14
Ghostwriter For Hire

I might do very well following the money trail. I want to make big hits and make some big sales. I have plenty of hot rhymes. I'm offering them wholesale. I'm a Ghost Writer for hire. I might take you higher.

Go ahead, shine brighter. Money should come proper. Guaranteed satisfaction, I'll push your work farther. Success might come faster. I'm always going harder to make a bigger splasher. Over and over, I want to make new bangers. I want them to be meaner; have the crowd in fever. I am a good performer and a crowd-pleaser. I keep doing it better. I have the desire to grow even stronger. I'll keep it ever clever. There's another matter. No matter the weather. Whether it's winter or summer, like the mailman carrier, I am out to deliver.

I am a music lover and a gifted composer.

You could be a top seller; I am your money maker. All the topics I cover. I do all music genres. If you're a good listener, you'll turn into a believer. You'll feel the strength and power of my music like thunder. My impact does last longer. Similar to a razor my lyrics do cut deeper. I am a practitioner, modern-day inventor, engineer, or producer. Like a time traveler, I'll spread my work all over, even in the near future. Similar to a trailer or even a tracker, my workload is heavier. I am a professional of a higher caliber. Label me the pathfinder. My lyrics are major. I'm the overachiever working on a new chapter. My reward, I am after. I am the right collector. I'm a better game-changer with lyrics that take over.

I'm looking forward to your reply.